I LVE
KINGS &
QUEENS

First published 2016.

Pitkin Publishing
The History Press
The Mill, Brimscombe Port
Stroud, Gloucestershire GL5 2QG
www.thehistorypress.co.uk

Enquiries and sales: 01453 883300
Email: sales@thehistorypress.co.uk

Text written by Richard Smyth.
The author has asserted their moral rights.

Designed by Chris West.

British Library Cataloguing in Publication Data.
A Catalogue record for this book is available from the British Library.

Publication in this form © Pitkin Publishing 2016.

ISBN 978-1-84165-695-3 1/16

Contents

		Facts
CHAPTER ONE:	Crowns, Children and Coronations	1 - 41
CHAPTER TWO:	Love, Marriage and Family	42 - 85
CHAPTER THREE:	War, Murder and Peril	86 - 146
CHAPTER FOUR:	Royal Characters	147 - 288
CHAPTER FIVE:	Religion, Politics and Money	289 - 343
CHAPTER SIX:	Mistresses, Bastards and Pretenders	344 - 369
CHAPTER SEVEN:	The King is Dead - Long Live the King!	370 - 400

CHAPTER ONE

Crowns, Children and Coronations

1 On 6 January 1066, Harold II became the first English king to be crowned in Westminster Abbey.

2 William the Conqueror (pictured) was next, crowned at Westminster on Christmas Day of 1066.

3 At the Conqueror's coronation, his soldiers mistook the crowd's shouts of acclamation for the outbreak of a riot and, in response, set fire to the surrounding buildings. William I's coronation was concluded amid billows of grey smoke, with the king allegedly trembling in terror.

4 On his ascent to the throne in 1154, Henry II (pictured) became the first undisputed king of England in more than 100 years.

5 Henry II made his son Henry king whilst he was still alive, and crowned him not once but twice – so two kings, one young and one old, ruled England at the same time, the only time in British history this has happened.

6 Even more weirdly, the two kings were not Henry II and Henry III – they were Henry II and the Young King. (The man we know as 'Henry III' was the Young King's nephew – whose name was also Henry!)

7 Henry III (pictured) was crowned in 1216 with a bracelet belonging to his mother: his father, King John, had managed to lose the Crown Jewels in quicksand while crossing the Wash (the large bay that separates East Anglia from Lincolnshire).

8 At just nine years of age, Henry III was the first boy-king to be crowned in England since Æthelred the Unready in 978.

9 Henry III was obsessed with Edward the Confessor. His decision to name his first son 'Edward' in homage seemed preposterous to the Norman aristocracy, who considered 'Edward' as foolishly archaic as Æthelwulf or Egbert.

10 On the birth of Edward I in 1239, Henry III inspected all gifts sent by well-wishers to the Royal Family, returning those he felt were not up to scratch with instructions to send something better.

11 At Edward II's (pictured) coronation on 25 February 1308, the king's notorious favourite Piers Gaveston scandalised the peers by wearing royal purple.

12 The press of the crowd at Edward II's coronation was such that a wall collapsed, crushing the noble Sir John Bakewell to death.

13 Under Edward III, royal babies came thick and fast. John, the sixth child of Edward and Philippa of Hainault, was born just ten years after the first – in the Belgian city of Ghent, hence 'John of Gaunt'.

14 The reign of the boy-king Richard II (pictured) began in 1377 with a dazzlingly lavish coronation ceremony. Richard was showered with flakes of gold, and, in parts of London, the water-pipes ran with wine.

15 Henry IV claimed that his ancestor, Edmund 'Crouchback', had been cruelly shunted aside in the succession because of his physical deformity. However, later historians dismissed this as nonsense.

KING HENRY THE V.ᵗʰ

16

On his accession to the throne in 1413, Henry V (pictured) ruled that none of the companions of his younger days should be allowed within ten miles of him.

17

Later writers claimed that Londoners cheered Richard III's coronation procession on 6 July 1483 half-heartedly, 'more for fear than for love'.

18 Henry Tudor – later Henry VII, founder of the Tudor dynasty – was conceived when his mother was just twelve years old.

19 Henry, the second son of Henry VII, was a talented child. In October 1494, aged just three, he rode unassisted from London to Westminster in order to be knighted by his father. The horsey boy grew up to be Henry VIII.

20 At her coronation, on 1 October 1553, Mary I (pictured) wore a jewelled diadem that was so heavy she had to hold her head up with her hands.

21

Elizabeth I's spectacular coronation on 15 January 1559 cost £16,741 (excluding the cost of the coronation banquet) – roughly equivalent to £3.5 million today.

22

For some 200 years, the people of England celebrated a public holiday on 17 November, the date of Elizabeth I's accession to the throne (and also the date of the death of her half-sister, Mary I).

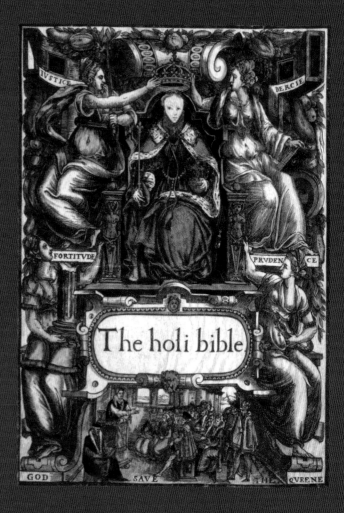

23

James I (pictured) of England did not set foot in England until the age of thirty-seven.

24

The son of Mary Queen of Scots, James became king of both countries in 1603. This made him the ruler of the largest kingdom ruled by a monarch in England since Oswy in the seventh century.

25

On his way from Scotland to London, King James called in on one of his loyal supporters, Sir Oliver Cromwell. A few decades later Sir Oliver's nephew, another Oliver, would order the execution of James's son Charles I.

26

Charles II (pictured) insisted on dating the beginning of his reign from the execution of his father. By this measure, his reign – usually reckoned at twenty-five years – should be considered a reign of forty-four years, as long as that of Elizabeth I.

27 When Mary of Modena, wife of the Catholic king James II, gave birth to a male heir in 1688, Protestant witnesses invited to attend at the baby's birth turned their backs. A rumour was then circulated that a foundling baby had been smuggled into the royal residence in a warming-pan.

28 Georg Ludwig, the Protestant elector of Hanover, was only fifty-second in line to the throne when Queen Anne died in 1714, but, according to the Act of Settlement, he was the nearest Protestant – and so he became king.

29 At the age of fifty-four, George I (pictured) was (at the time) the oldest person ever to take the throne.

30 George I (his name was Anglicised) was proclaimed king of England on 1 August 1714, but remained at home in Hanover until 18 September. For the intervening six weeks, England was in effect ruled from abroad.

At the coronation of George II (pictured) in October 1727, choristers were heard to sing two completely different anthems at the same time.

32 George II was the last British monarch to have been born outside Great Britain.

33

On 25 October 1760, George, son of Frederick, Prince of Wales, received a note written on a rough piece of brown paper. It read simply 'Schroeder' – the agreed code-word that told him his grandfather, George II, was dying and that he was about to become king. He took the throne as George III (pictured).

34

George III's queen, Charlotte of Mecklenburg-Strelitz, went into labour with the couple's first child on 12 August 1762. The excited king declared a huge reward: £500 to whoever brought him news of a baby daughter, but £1,000 for a baby boy.

When the child was born, the Earl of Huntingdon, Master of the King's Horse, rushed to the king's chambers to give him the news – that George was the father of a healthy baby daughter! In fact, the child was a boy – the future George IV.

A royal birth had to be closely scrutinised to ensure its legitimacy. Charlotte of Mecklenburg-Strelitz (pictured) gave birth in the company of her German lady attendants and the Ladies of the Bedchamber, the First Lord of the Treasury, the two Secretaries of State, the officers of the Privy Council, the officers of the Royal Household and the Archbishop of Canterbury!

37 Queen Victoria's first child, Edward, was the first heir born to a reigning monarch since George IV in 1762, and the last to be born in the presence of the Privy Council.

38 Edward VII (pictured) was fifty-nine years old when he became king in 1901, having been heir apparent for longer than any other monarch in British history.

39 At Edward VII's coronation in August 1902, his numerous mistresses – past and present – were accommodated in an area irreverently dubbed 'the loose box'.

40 When, in 1952, Elizabeth II acceded to the throne, she was up a giant fig-tree in east Africa. She and her husband Philip were spending the night at Treetops Hotel in Kenya – a lodge built in the branches of a 300-year-old fig – when George VI died in his sleep.

41 Elizabeth (pictured on the right) was the first British monarch since George I to accede to the throne while overseas.

CHAPTER
TWO

Love,
Marriage
and Family

42 Edward the Elder, the son of Alfred the Great, was the first king of all England. He had three wives (or possibly two wives and one mistress) and fathered five sons and at least ten daughters.

43 Edward the Confessor (pictured) was married to Edith, the daughter of Earl Godwine of Essex. For religious reasons, however, their marriage was never consummated.

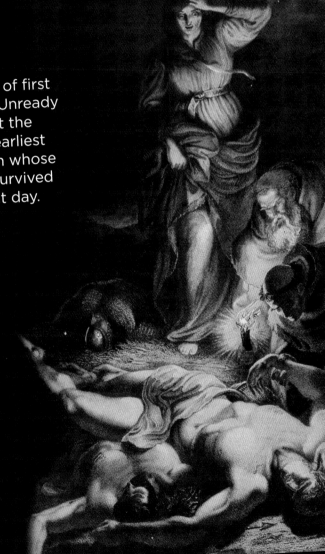

44

Emma, queen of first Æthelred the Unready and then Cnut the Great, is the earliest English queen whose portrait has survived to the present day.

45

Harold II had the name of his wife, another Edith, tattooed across his heart. After his gruesome death at the Battle of Hastings (actually fought at Senlac), the king's tats were used to help identify his body.

46

William the Conqueror's formidable wife Matilda of Flanders was once known as 'that strange woman'. By the time of her death in 1083, however, she was being hailed as 'Queen Matilda, wealthy and powerful'.

47

One night in 1237, a knife-wielding madman broke into the bedchamber of Edward III and aimed a lethal thrust at the king's bed. Luckily, the king wasn't there – he was in the bedchamber of his thirteen-year-old wife, Eleanor of Castile.

48 Henry III married Eleanor of Provence when she was twelve. At twenty-nine, he was more than twice her age.

49 Henry VI (pictured) was notoriously uninterested in sex. When one aristocrat put on a show for him of 'young ladies with bared bosoms', Henry turned away, crying, 'Fie! Fie! For shame!'

50 In 1464, the lusty Edward IV (pictured) caused a scandal by contracting a secret marriage with the beautiful Lancastrian widow Elizabeth Woodville. It is said that he proposed when he realised it was the only way of bedding her.

51 Edward IV's daughter, Elizabeth of York, was the model for the first 'queen' found in a deck of cards.

52 Elizabeth married Henry VII in 1486. Among the wedding gifts sent to the new queen was a pair of clavichords, thought to be the first keyboards ever seen in England.

53

In 1505, aged forty-eight, widower Henry VII despatched two envoys to Italy to investigate the young widow Joanna of Naples, who was just twenty-five, with a view to marriage. The royal checklist included the length of Joanna's neck (which was 'comely, not misshapen, nor very short nor very long'), whether she was 'fat or lean, sharp or round' ('somewhat round and fat'), the size of her breasts ('somewhat great and full') and whether she had any hair on her upper lip ('she hath none').

54 Henry VIII struggled to produce male heirs, fathering only one legitimate son in the course of his six marriages. But it was not only his fertility that was sometimes in doubt: Anne Boleyn, Henry's doomed second wife, noted that the king had 'neither talent nor vigour' between the sheets.

55 Henry VIII dismissed Anne of Cleves as 'a Flanders mare'.

56 Charles II, on first seeing Catherine of Braganza's hair (which was black and styled, after the Portuguese fashion, in projecting ringlets), exclaimed: 'They have brought me a bat!'

57 Mary II is said to have wept for a day and a half on learning that she was to be married to William of Orange, the future William III.

58 George III realised that members of the Royal Family cannot always be relied upon to marry wisely: the Royal Marriages Act (1772) states that the wife of any lineal descendant of George II must be approved by the sovereign. It was only repealed in 2015.

59

George IV's marriage to Caroline of Brunswick was apparently doomed from the off. His first words on seeing his future queen in April 1795 were, 'I am not well. Pray get me a glass of brandy!'

Yes your Injured Wife

60 Nor was Caroline particularly impressed by the louche, heavy-drinking Prince of Wales. She later reported that she found him 'very stout and by no means as handsome as his portrait.'

61 The Duke of Clarence, later William IV, enjoyed twenty years of domestic bliss with his mistress Dorothy Bland (famous on the London stage as 'Mrs' Jordan) before he married.

62 Between 1794 and 1807, Dorothy bore the future king William IV five sons and five daughters. In 1818 he married Princess Adelaide of Saxe-Meiningen, but the match produced no legitimate heirs.

63 Queen Victoria and her beloved husband Albert appear in the 1851 Census. Albert (pictured) is identified as the 'Head of the Household', while Victoria, further down the form, gives her occupation as 'The Queen'.

64 Mary of Teck, the wife of George V, was previously engaged to George's brother, Prince Albert Victor, before he died of pneumonia in 1892.

65 Queen Mary (pictured) was an inch taller than her husband George V.

66 Elizabeth II, like Victoria, considered her husband the head of the royal household, and in her wedding vows promised to obey him. However, while Victoria's marriage saw the House of Hanover become the House of Saxe-Coburg-Gotha, the family name remains 'Windsor' rather than 'Mountbatten'.

67 Elfrida, queen of Edgar the Peaceable, was notorious in Anglo-Saxon England. She was believed to have murdered both her first husband, Æthelwold, and her second husband's son, Edward 'the Martyr'.

68 Fulbert, the grandfather of William the Conqueror, was a skinner by trade. When enemy troops at the siege of Alençon made fun of William by waving skins and furs at him, William had their hands and feet cut off.

69 Henry II was the first English king of the House of Plantagenet. Geoffrey of Anjou, Henry's father, took to wearing a sprig of broom flower (his adopted emblem) in his hat. The broom flower had the Latin name *Planta genista*.

70 Family disputes can get serious when kings are involved and kingdoms are at stake. In 1203, a drunken, wrathful King John murdered his nephew Arthur of Brittany with his own hands. John had previously ordered that the youth be blinded and castrated, but Arthur's gaoler balked at the brutality.

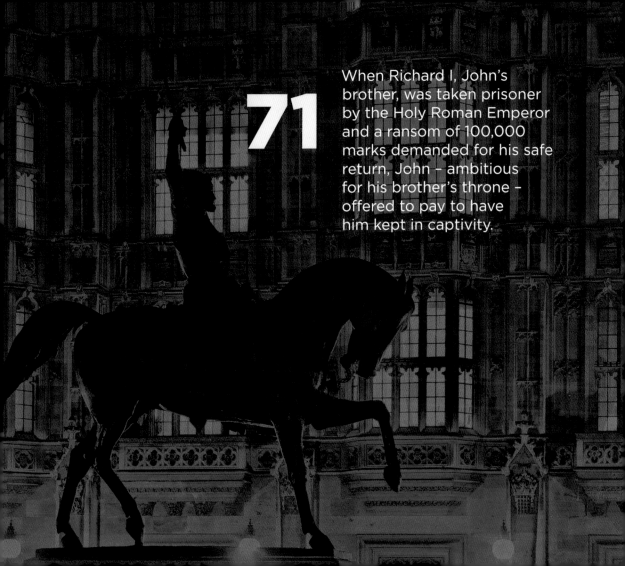

71

When Richard I, John's brother, was taken prisoner by the Holy Roman Emperor and a ransom of 100,000 marks demanded for his safe return, John – ambitious for his brother's throne – offered to pay to have him kept in captivity.

72 The House of Stuart expired as an English royal dynasty with the death of Queen Anne, but the family line is not quite extinguished. Franz, the elderly Duke of Bavaria, is Charles I's great-great-great-great-great-great-great-great-great-grandson.

73 George I despised both his son George II and George's wife, Caroline of Brandenburg-Ansbach. When their first son, Frederick, was born, the king refused to pay for any celebrations.

74 Caroline, in her turn, grew to loathe her son Frederick. On one occasion, encountering Frederick in the grounds of St James' Palace, she declared, 'Look, there he goes – that wretch! – that villain! – I wish the ground would open this moment and sink the monster to the lowest hole in hell!'

75 Another time, Queen Caroline told the minister Robert Walpole that Frederick – her son, remember – had 'the most vicious nature and false heart that ever man had'. His vices were not those of a gentleman, she added, but 'the mean, base tricks of a knavish footman.'

76 Queen Victoria (pictured), the granddaughter of German George III, was half-German on her mother's side. She married a German and spoke German with him at home - she even spoke English with a mild German accent.

77 'I had a very unhappy childhood,' Victoria once said. Her mother raised her using the 'Kensington System': she was watched twenty-four hours a day, denied friends of her own, and was never allowed to be alone. She was also made to sleep in her mother's bedroom.

78 Victoria's first act on becoming queen was to ask for an hour alone.

79

Victoria was to have nine children, but her first experience of pregnancy was not to her liking. 'If I have a nasty girl at the end of my plagues,' she wrote while expecting her first child, 'I shall drown it!' It was a girl, but fortunately she didn't carry out her threat.

80

Victoria's son and successor Edward VII (pictured on the right) spoke German with his siblings and retained a German accent throughout his life.

81

Edward VII was related to nearly every Continental sovereign and came to be known as the 'Uncle of Europe'.

82 Kaiser Wilhelm (pictured) was George V's first cousin.

83 Charles, Queen Victoria's grandson, was stripped of his titles in 1919 for taking the Kaiser's side in the First World War. He later went on to join the Nazi Party.

84 George V pithily summed up the stern parenting traditions of the Hanoverian monarchy when he said, of his two sons, 'my father was scared of his father, I was scared of my father, and I'm damn well going to see that they're scared of me.'

85 George V is also reported to have said of his son Edward: 'After I am dead, the boy will ruin himself in 12 months.' Small wonder that Edward, having abdicated the throne in order to marry Wallis Simpson, later remarked: 'What impresses me most about America is the way parents obey their children.'

CHAPTER
THREE

War,
Murder
and Peril

86 King Edmund of East Anglia was captured by the Viking leader Ivarr the Boneless in 869. When the king refused to renounce his Christian faith, Ivarr had Edmund tied to a tree and ordered his archers to use him for target practice.

87 The Vikings then cut off King Edmund's head and chucked it into the forest – where, according to legend, it was found by a wolf. The wolf is supposed to have led Edmund's men to the spot by calling out 'here, here, here!'

88

At Maserfield in 641 (or possibly 642) the forces of pagan Mercia, under their chieftain Penda, crushed the Northumbrians. The Northumbrian king, Oswald, was captured, dismembered and hung from a tree. The incident is thought to be the source of the name of the town of Oswestry, from 'Oswald's tree'.

89

Æthelfleda, daughter of Alfred the Great and the 'Lady of the Mercians', was the only Anglo-Saxon queen ever to lead her troops into battle.

90

Although, like her father, she never ruled England as a whole, Æthelfleda was the country's last successful and enduring female ruler until the accession of Elizabeth I in 1558.

91

In 946, the Anglo-Saxon king Edmund I, 'The Magnificent', was dining at a banquet when he spotted a man who was supposed to have been exiled. Edmund ordered the man's arrest – but, in the ensuing struggle, the king was fatally stabbed. He was just twenty-five.

92

The death of Edmund II ('Ironside') in 1016 has long been attributed to an intimate wound from a spear thrust upwards as he was sitting on the toilet. The truth is probably less colourful (and less gruesome): it's more likely that Edmund perished from wounds sustained in battle against Cnut's Vikings.

93

Edmund II's decision to ally with the treacherous Earl Eadric in 1016 was described in the Anglo-Saxon Chronicle as the worst decision ever made for the English nation.

94 The best evidence suggests that an arrow did not kill Harold II at Hastings: instead, he was probably cut down in battle by a troop of Norman knights.

95 It's thought that one of the knights at Hastings mutilated King Harold's corpse so horribly that William the Conqueror had him drummed out of the army.

96 When dressing for battle on the day of the Battle of Hastings, William, Duke of Normandy – very soon to be William the Conqueror – put his 'hauberk' or mail-shirt on backwards.

97

During the Battle of Hastings, William had three horses killed under him.

98

William I was a soldier of formidable reputation. While at 5ft 10in he was no match in physical stature for rivals such as the giant Harald Hardrada of Norway, it was said that William could bend on horseback a bow that a normal man couldn't bend standing on solid ground.

99 William 'Rufus', the son and successor of the Conqueror, was also a redoubtable fighter. He mostly fought against his own brother, Robert Curthose of Normandy.

100 Modesty was not a royal virtue in William Rufus's time. Crossing the Channel to confront his brother while a severe storm was threatening, he scoffed: 'I never heard of a king being drowned; you will see the elements join to obey me!'

101 During the civil war – often dubbed 'the Anarchy' – that followed the death of Henry I, Henry's daughter Matilda was forced to escape from Devizes castle wrapped in a shroud and disguised as a corpse.

102

At Lincoln in 1141, Stephen of Blois – Matilda's rival for the throne – had a couple of unlucky breaks: first his sword broke in two, and then his battle-axe snapped.

103

King Stephen was finally captured by a soldier who hit him on the head with a rock and shouted: 'Here! I've got the king!'

Henry II's reign was marred by the bloody murder in Canterbury Cathedral of Thomas Becket, the Archbishop of Canterbury. Henry's 'troublesome priest' speech is a myth.
He actually said: 'What miserable drones and traitors have I nourished in my household, who let their lord be treated with such shameful contempt by a low-born clerk!?'

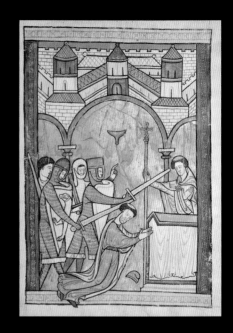

The soldier-king Richard I was so hell-bent on conquest and Crusade that even severe illness couldn't keep him from the field. In 1191, he contracted a disease called 'arnaldia', which caused all his hair and fingernails to fall out. Nevertheless, he continued to direct manoeuvres at the siege of Acre.

106 In 1189-90, Richard spent £14,000 on a stockpile of Crusading provisions that included 14,000 pig carcasses and 60,000 horseshoes.

107 Richard met his death in the field, but not at the hands of a great warrior. Peter Basilius, the man who fired the crossbow-bolt that killed the king, did so while wielding a frying-pan as a makeshift shield.

108 The greatest rebel of Henry III's reign, Simon de Montfort, was killed in battle in 1265. He was subsequently dismembered. His head was cut off and decorated with his severed genitals.

109 Edward I was famous for his close brushes with death. Once, as a youth, he was playing chess and had just risen to stretch his legs when a large lump of masonry fell from the ceiling and crushed his seat.

110 In 1297, at Winchelsea, a horse was spooked by a windmill and jumped over the high town ramparts, taking Edward I with it.

111 On Easter Sunday in 1286, Edward I and a number of nobles were in the highest room of a tower when the floor gave way. The company plummeted 80 feet to the ground; three knights were killed, but Edward sustained only a broken collarbone.

112

At Acre in 1172, on his thirty-third birthday, Edward I was attacked in his chambers by an undercover assassin sent by his Mamluk enemy Baybars. He bested the assassin – with first a punch and then a knife-blow to the head – but was stabbed in the hip with a poisoned blade.

113

According to legend, either his wife Eleanor or his friend Otto de Grandson sucked the poison from Edward I's wound.

114 At Bannockburn in 1314 – perhaps his greatest humiliation – Edward II had to be dragged from the battlefield by the great knight Sir Giles d'Argenteine (who was hacked to death on returning to the fray).

115 As the Hundred Years War with France built up steam under Edward III, the royal lodgings in St Thomas's Tower (part of the Tower of London) were used as storage rooms for armour and crossbows.

116 A young Henry V fought at the Battle of Shrewsbury in 1403 – he was just sixteen at the time.

117 Shrewsbury was the first battle fought on English soil in which two armies of longbowmen faced each other. Henry V could not dodge the arrow-storm: he was struck in the face by an arrow that penetrated his cheek to a depth of 6in.

118 Henry VI, Henry V's unfortunate son, was the first English king since the Norman Conquest never to have commanded an army.

119 During the second battle of St Albans in 1461, Henry – who was plagued in the later years of his reign by mental illness – sat under a tree, singing to himself.

120

Richard III, usually held responsible for the disappearance of the 'Princes in the Tower', is also the chief suspect in the murders of Henry VI and his young son, Prince Edward.

121

The fatal order may in fact have come from Richard III's brother, Edward IV.

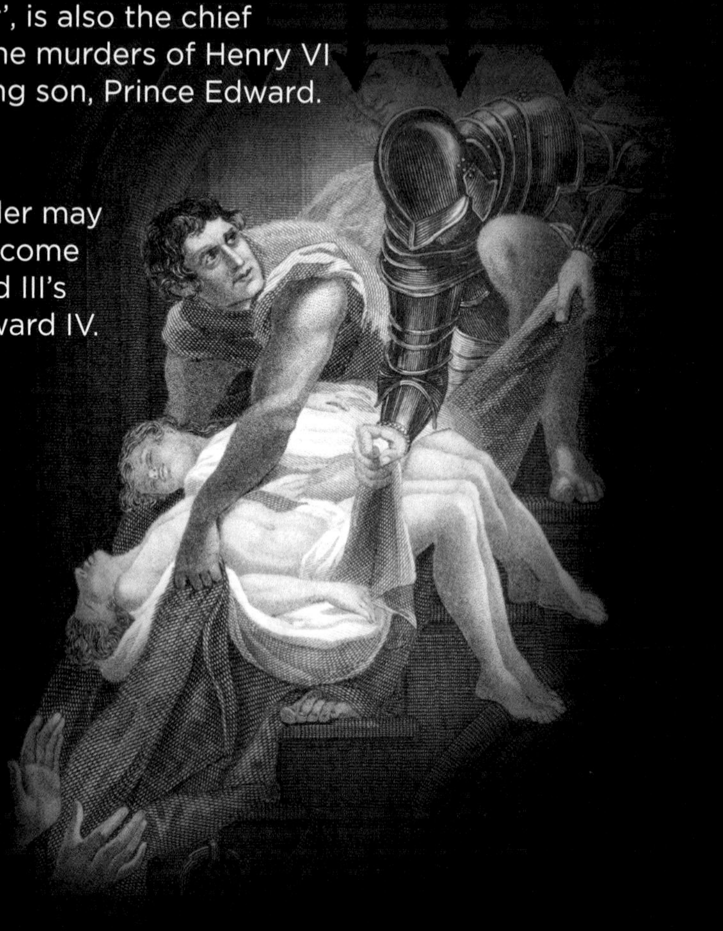

122 Richard III was killed at the battle of Bosworth in 1485. In 1813 his supporters erected a plaque to mark the spot where 'King Richard fell fighting gallantly in defence of his realm and his crown against the usurper Henry Tudor'.

123 The personal bodyguard known as the 'Yeomen of the Guard' (pictured) established by Henry Tudor – later Henry VII – on his seizure of the throne is now the oldest military corps in existence.

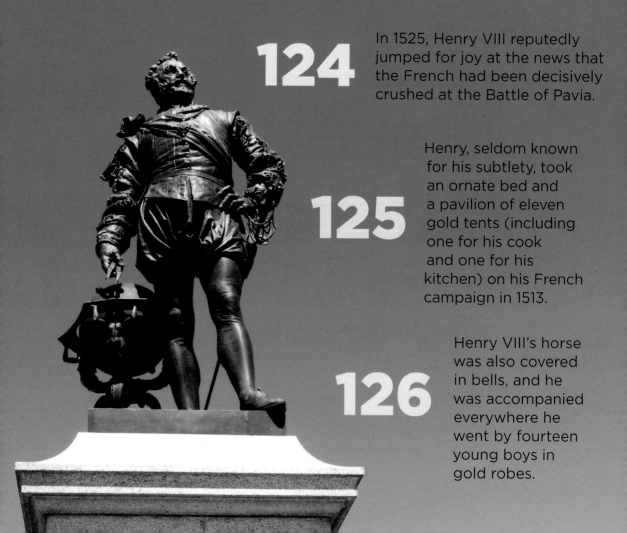

124

In 1525, Henry VIII reputedly jumped for joy at the news that the French had been decisively crushed at the Battle of Pavia.

125

Henry, seldom known for his subtlety, took an ornate bed and a pavilion of eleven gold tents (including one for his cook and one for his kitchen) on his French campaign in 1513.

126

Henry VIII's horse was also covered in bells, and he was accompanied everywhere he went by fourteen young boys in gold robes.

127 In January 1554, the retinue of Philip, Queen Mary I's Spanish husband-to-be, was pelted with snowballs by London urchins.

128 In 1584, the MP William Parry lay in wait for Elizabeth I with the aim of assassinating her – but, on her arrival, found himself so overwhelmed by the majesty of her regal presence that he was unable to go through with the deed. Elizabeth, majestically, had him executed.

129 The wars fought by Britain during Elizabeth I's reign are estimated to have cost more than £5 million, a sum that far outstripped Crown revenues.

130 For example, in 1588, the year in which Sir Francis Drake bested the Spanish Armada, Elizabeth's total annual revenue amounted to a piddling £392,000.

131 On 30 January 1649, King Charles I was led to the executioner's block. Charles was wearing two shirts against the cold, so it could never be said that the King of England trembled in the face of death.

Charles I's final words were: 'I go from a corruptible to an incorruptible Crown, where no disturbance can be.'

132

133 Charles II famously escaped capture by hiding up a tree (the 'Boscobel Oak') which stood in the middle of a field.

134 The oak was chosen because it was such a stupidly obvious hiding place that the Roundheads would never think to search it.

135 Other ploys that Charles II used to escape from the Parliamentarians included cutting off his hair and posing as a blacksmith.

136 Charles II was carried ashore to his exile in France on the shoulders of his ship's mate.

137 In June of 1743, the war-crazy George II led his troops into action at the Battle of Dettingen. It was the last time an English king led an army on the battlefield.

138 On 2 August 1786, 'a woman very decently dressed' attacked George III with an ivory-handled dessert knife. She got close enough to scrape his waistcoat. 'I am not hurt,' George said. 'Take care of the woman; do not hurt her, for she is mad.'

139 George III's would-be-assassin, Margaret Nicholson, claimed to be the rightful ruler of England, and declared that, if she was not crowned queen, 'England would drown in blood for a thousand generations'.

140 Another religious maniac, an army veteran named James Hadfield who had received several sabre-blows to the head in battle, took a shot at George in a theatre in 1800. He missed by inches; the bullet lodged in a pillar of the royal box.

141 In court, it was revealed that the would-be assassin believed that his own death at the hands of the State would bring about the second coming of Christ.

142 In June 1832, a stone thrown by a protestor at Ascot struck William IV on the head. The extra padding he'd packed into his hat to keep it from falling off proved a life-saver.

143 The curious shape of William IV's head – which was often likened to a pineapple or coconut – was a source of much merriment for his less reverent subjects throughout his reign.

144 Seven attempts were made on Queen Victoria's life between 1840 and 1882.

145 George V (pictured) served for several years as a naval officer. Setting the tone for generations of royals to come, he once remarked: 'We sailors never smile when on duty.'

146 His son, George VI, made a different sort of contribution to the British war effort. During the Second World War, the frugal king personally marked the 5in water limit on the bathtubs of Buckingham Palace.

CHAPTER FOUR

Royal Characters

147 William 'Rufus' (pictured) was short, thick-set and muscular, with a fat belly, but indisputably a dandy: his short tunics and curling, pointed shoes attracted criticism from conservative contemporaries.

148 His byname 'Rufus' referred either to the king's strawberry-blond hair (parted, daringly, in the middle) or his red face.

149 Rufus swore like a trooper, though not in forms that we would recognise as obscene. His favourite oaths were obscure and puzzling even at the time: he was well-known for exclaiming 'By the holy face of Lucca!' or 'By the mountains and valleys!' at moments of exasperation.

150 Henry I's byname 'Beauclerc' reflected his good education. Henry (pictured) may have been the first Norman king to be fluent in English.

151 Henry II, however, didn't speak English, and spent only a third of his reign in England.

152 Henry II was extremely energetic and seldom sat down. 'He would wear the whole court out by continually standing,' wrote the chronicler Gerald of Wales.

153

Henry II's vigour amazed
his contemporaries too:
the French king remarked,
'Now in England, now
in Normandy, he must
fly rather than travel
by horse or ship.'

154

Henry II was known for his
fearsome temper. In one of his
rages, triggered by a complimentary
remark someone let slip about the
king of Scotland, Henry 'fell out of
bed screaming, tore up his coverlet,
and threshed around on the floor, cramming
his mouth with the stuffing of his mattress.'

155 King John was also subject to Plantagenet rages. In 1208 he pledged to pluck out the eyeballs and slice out the tongues of the Pope's envoys.

156 John's son Henry III stood around 5'6" and was distinguished by a drooping eyelid.

157 Henry's son, Edward I, was 6ft 2in – hence his byname 'Longshanks' – and spoke with a lisp.

158 As a youth, Edward I was known as 'the Leopard' because of his slyness.

159 He, too, exhibited the Plantagenet temper: during one particularly fierce outburst he was said to have literally frightened a man to death.

160 On another occasion his fury was such that he tore out his son's hair in clumps.

161 In 1290 he was required to pay 20 marks in compensation to a man he had assaulted with a stick, and in 1297 he flung his daughter Elizabeth's coronet into a fire.

162 Edward III (pictured) was the first king to leave us samples of his handwriting.

163 Edward III was subject to bouts of dysentery. One doctor prescribed him a medicinal paste of ambergris, musk, pearls, gold and silver, which cost £134, equivalent to the yearly income of three noblemen.

164 The terms of address 'Your Highness' and 'Your Majesty' were introduced to England under the reign of Richard II. Previously, monarchs had made do with 'my lord'.

165 Richard II had a personal retinue of tough Cheshire archers and men-at-arms, who addressed him as 'Dickon' – roughly equivalent to 'Dickie' or 'Richie'.

166 Henry IV cultivated a tremendous beard. When his tomb was opened in 1832, the beard was still going strong; it was reported to be 'thick and matted, and of a deep russet colour'.

167 In later years, Henry IV suffered from a severe skin complaint that is believed to have been either leprosy or acute dermatitis. At the time, many suggested it was divine retribution for Henry's usurpation of the throne.

168

Edward IV was a glutton in every sense. He could be bloodthirsty on the battlefield; Thomas More noted that in his youth he was 'greatly given to fleshy wantonness'; during banquets, he was known to make himself vomit in order to make more room for further gorging.

169

Henry VI experienced a severe mental breakdown in the summer of 1453. At first he became hysterical; then he suffered a physical collapse. During the seventeen-month stupor that followed, the king had to be spoon-fed. It seemed, one chronicler wrote, that 'his wit and reson [were] withdrawen'.

170 The Spanish diplomat Pedro de Ayala wrote of Henry VII that 'one of the reasons why he lives a good life is that he has been brought up abroad'.

171 Henry VIII did not age well. An athletic sportsman as a youth, by 1541 he had bloated dramatically: his waist measured 54in, and his chest 57in.

172 In later years, Henry VIII travelled in a 'tram' or primitive wheelchair, wore glasses or 'gazings' clipped to his nose, and 'could not go up or down stairs unless he was raised up or let down by an engine'.

173 Henry VIII spent large sums on rhubarb, which was believed to be a remedy for illnesses in men of a 'choleric' – i.e bad-tempered – nature.

174 Edward VI (pictured) was famous as a boy for his scholarly accomplishments. His memory was practically photographic; it was said, for instance, that he could list every creek, bay, and rivulet in England, Scotland and France.

175 Elizabeth I sometimes referred to herself as 'the Lion's cub', alluding to her father, Henry VIII, 'the Lion'.

176 Despite her love of travelling in glorious procession around her realm, Elizabeth I never travelled further north than Stafford.

At the age of forty-five, Elizabeth I suffered a bout of toothache that kept her from sleep for forty-eight hours. A tooth-puller was summoned, but the queen refused to undergo the procedure until the Bishop of London volunteered to have one of his own teeth pulled out to prove that it was safe.

178

In 1572, the Earl of Leicester presented Elizabeth I with the world's first-ever wristwatch.

179 Elizabeth I was understandably sensitive about the image she presented to her people. In 1596, she ordered the seizure of all paintings in which she looked ill, old, or weak.

180 In 1597, at the age of sixty-four, Elizabeth was described by the French ambassador as 'very aged ... her teeth are very yellow and unequal... Many of them are missing so that one cannot understand her easily when she speaks.'

181 In 1603, at the age of sixty-nine, Elizabeth looked in a mirror for the first time in twenty years. It cannot have been a pleasant experience.

182 Approached as a possible husband for England's virgin queen, Henry, Duke of Anjou, rejected Elizabeth I as 'an old creature with a sore leg'. She had developed a leg ulcer like those that had so severely plagued her father.

183 In 1613, Dr De Mayerne, court physician to James I, made the troubling observation that His Majesty's urine was often a vivid purple – 'the colour of Alicante wine'.

184 Charles I stood only 5ft 4in tall. He suffered from weak ankles (as a result of childhood rickets) and a pronounced stutter, but was nevertheless a charismatic speaker.

185 Mary II – at a commanding 5ft 11in – was five inches taller than her Dutch husband, William III.

186 William's unflattering nicknames among his subjects included 'Hook Nose' and 'the Rotten Orange'.

187 Six of Queen Anne's seven brothers and sisters died in infancy. Anne (pictured) herself gave birth to eighteen children, none of which survived her.

188 George II – though not a Plantagenet – was prone to outbursts of temper. On such occasions he was wont to tear off his wig, fling it to the floor, and kick it around the room in frustration.

189

On his recovery from mental illness in 1789, George III received 756 congratulatory addresses from groups of relieved subjects.

190

George III's well-documented mental illness once resulted in a premature declaration of his death. During a walk at Kew, the king, always a reluctant patient, sat down on the grass and refused to move. When he lay down prostrate, he was spotted by a curious passer-by – and the rumour spread that George was dead.

191 George III was eventually carried home, still stubbornly lying horizontal, on his attendants' shoulders.

192 When George died in 1820, he was very nearly followed by his son and heir. The newly-declared George IV suffered a severe attack of pleurisy just two days after the old king's passing, and was said by his doctors to be 'in imminent danger' of death; he was too ill to attend his father's funeral.

193 George IV's 'treatment' included the letting of 150 fluid ounces (about four litres) of blood.

194 In later life, George IV was too obese and ridden with gout to mount a horse by himself. When he was required to ride, he had to be wheeled up a ramp and hoisted into the saddle from a high platform.

195 William IV was in many ways a genial, good-natured king. On his birthday he threw a banquet for 3,000 of the poorer inhabitants of Windsor.

196 As patriotic as his subjects, one of William IV's first acts as king was to dismiss George IV's French cooks and German musicians and replace them with (less talented) English equivalents.

197 Queen Victoria's personal physician, John Snow, gave her a controversial new super-drug called 'chloroform' to numb pain during the birth of her eighth child, Leopold; she described the drug as 'soothing, quieting & delightful beyond measure'.

198

Victoria was merciless with regard to the physical shortcomings of her son 'Bertie', the future Edward VII. 'His nose and mouth are too enormous,' she wrote, 'and he pastes his hair down to his head, and wears his clothes frightfully. He really is anything but good-looking.'

199

Edward VII became known in his social circle – though not, of course, to his face – as 'Tum Tum', on account of his increasing portliness.

200

George V had a red-and-green dragon tattooed on his arm, a souvenir from a visit to a Japanese tattoo parlour during his stint in the navy.

201

In stark contrast to his forebears, George considered German 'a rotten language, which I find very difficult'.

202

During the First World War, George V reluctantly took 'the King's Pledge', vowing to abstain from alcohol for the duration of the conflict.

203 George V (pictured) suffered from terrible headaches as a result of his dutiful insistence on wearing the crown – which was a poor fit for his head – at ceremonial events.

204 It's thought that George V was the first English monarch since the Norman Conquest to speak no language other than English.

205 George VI was naturally left-handed but was forced by his parents and tutors to write with his right hand.

206 In his final exams at school, George VI finished sixty-eighth out of sixty-nine.

207 In one year, Charles I (pictured) bought 513 pairs of boots, shoes or slippers.

208 Just one of Mary I's nightgowns used 15 yards of satin-lined black velvet, 12 yards of fur-lined black damask lined with 3 more yards of black velvet.

209 At a wedding in 1311, Isabella of France, wife of Edward II, sported a girdle covered with 300 rubies and 1,800 pearls.

210 The handkerchief was the ingenious invention of Richard II, who also popularised the codpiece, the high-necked houpelande robe, and shoes so long and pointy they had to be fastened to the knee by a garter.

211

Elizabeth I dressed so lavishly that tiny seed-pearls tumbled from her clothes whenever she moved.

212

King John (pictured) indulged his queen Isabella's love for fine Lucca silk, buying her a tunic, fifteen gowns, thirty pairs of stockings, four cloaks, six bodices and thirty-six pairs of shoes in just one year.

213

Between 1608 and 1613, meanwhile, James I bought almost 2,000 pairs of gloves and 180 suits.

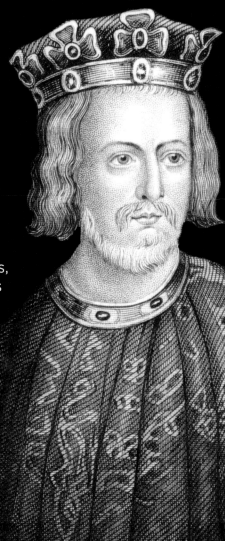

214 Henry I – a keen huntsman, like many of his successors – was nicknamed 'Stagfoot' because he was reputed to be able to tell from a stag's tracks how many antlers it had.

215 Henry II employed a fool called 'Roland the Farter' who specialised in breaking wind for the king's amusement.

216 Richard I was said to have brought home a crocodile from his travels abroad – only for the animal to escape into the Thames.

217 King John was the first English monarch to have been portrayed on stage, in John Bale's 'Kynge Johan', and the first English king to adopt the 'three lions' for his royal seal.

218 John was also a big fan of taking baths – he took a remarkable eight baths in the first six months of 1209 – and was the first king to wear a bathrobe.

219 During Henry III's reign, a menagerie of beasts including lions, a polar bear and an elephant – all gifts from foreign rulers – were kept at the Tower of London.

220 Prepping ingredients for his 1251 Christmas feast, Henry III put out an order for swans from across England. In the event, 351 swans were served up to the royal guests. That's about 3 tonnes of swan.

221

Edward I (pictured) employed a dancer named Matilda Makejoy.

222

Every Easter Monday, Edward I would challenge his wife's ladies-in-waiting to catch him in bed, offering a reward to any who succeeded.

223

Edward II employed a personal 'tumbler' who, for the entertainment of the court, would repeatedly fall off his horse for twenty shillings a tumble.

224

According to the legend, the name of the Order of the Garter comes from a racy incident with the Countess of Salisbury: Edward III replaced the lady's garter when it slipped off during a dance, gallantly murmuring, 'Honi soit qui mal y pense', or 'Evil be to he who evil thinks.'

225

However, the Order of the Garter's name really comes from the jewelled garters that Edward and his fellow bloods were wont to wear as younger men.

226 Edward III celebrated his fiftieth birthday in 1362 by recognising English as the official tongue of his kingdom.

227 Richard II commissioned the first royal cookery book. 'The Forme of Cury' contains 196 recipes for starters, mains and sweets, mostly cooked in expensive spices such as cardamom, cloves and ginger.

228 Richard was described in the prologue of the first English cookbook as 'the royallest viander' in Christendom.

229 Henry VI was an unsuccessful king, but a genuinely committed patron of culture and education: he was the founder of both the college of Eton and King's College at Cambridge University.

230

Henry VIII was a multilingual, multi-instrumentalist merry monarch. In 1515, for instance, he and his court marked May Day by dressing up as Robin Hood and his Merrie Men and having a banquet in a nearby forest.

231

Henry VIII was described by Giustinian in 1519 as an 'affable and gracious' man who 'harmed no-one'; Erasmus said that he was 'a man of gentle friendliness'.

232

Mary I was a demon at the card table. At one point, after 1536, the queen was spending nearly one-third of her allowance on gambling.

233

In July 1575, Elizabeth spent nineteen days with Robert Dudley, Earl of Leicester, at Kenilworth Castle (pictured opposite). Dudley's lavish hospitality cost around £1,000 per day.

234

The white makeup Elizabeth wore to cover her smallpox scars was a concoction of white lead and vinegar.

235

Her rouge was made from crushed cochineal beetles and she applied highly toxic mercuric sulphide to her lips.

236

In 1587, Elizabeth I's jewellery collection contained 628 pieces. On her death, she possessed some 2,000 dresses.

237 In 1617-18, James I published his 'Book of Sports' setting out the pastimes that his subjects were permitted to take part in on a Sunday (after they had been to church, of course).

238 Approved pastimes for Stuart subjects included 'dancing', 'Archerie for men', 'leaping', 'vaulting' and 'Morris-dances'.

239 Forbidden pursuits for Stuarts included bull-baiting, bear-baiting and bowling.

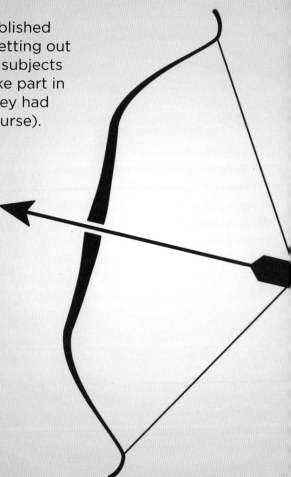

240

When James's son Charles I reissued the 'Book of Sports' in 1633, the poet John Milton (pictured) warned that it could lead to 'gaming, jigging, wassailing and mixt dancing'.

241

The 'Book of Sports' was publicly burned in 1643 on the orders of Parliament.

242 Charles II described the debates in the House of Lords as 'better than a play'.

243 Charles II was a cockfighting enthusiast, and built a cockfighting pit at Birdcage Walk in London.

244 Henry VIII once did the same, at Whitehall Palace. The building later became the Privy Council Office.

245 It was widely rumoured in the 1690s that the gay 'set' that grew up around the Duke of Shrewsbury also included William III and his page, Arnold van Keppel.

246 Mary II (pictured) was a great animal lover. Visitors to her gallery, which was bedecked with birdcages, had to take care not to trip over the little red velvet beds she had made for her dogs.

247
Eighteen months after her husband died in 1708, Queen Anne came to Kensington Palace with her intimate friend Sarah, Duchess of Marlborough. They were so close that – in defiance of court protocol – they called one another 'Mrs Morley' and 'Mrs Freeman'.

248
After a fierce argument at Kensington in 1710, Queen Anne and Sarah never met again; Sarah later accused the queen of having 'no liking for anyone but her own sex'.

249 Anne was zealously keen on hunting. Even the trauma of seventeen pregnancies, illness, obesity and old age could not keep her from racing after stags – although in later life she was forced to travel in a small carriage to do so.

250 Frederick, son of George II and father of George III, was, as a young man, a notorious prankster and roisterer who enjoyed nothing more than running around town with like-minded hoorays and breaking decent people's windows.

251 On one occasion, while prowling for female companionship in St James' Park, George II's son was robbed of his wallet, twenty-two guineas, and the Royal Seal.

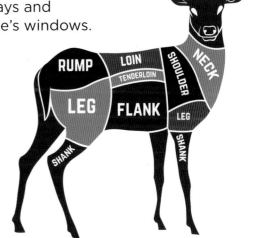

252 George III's deep and genuine interest in the practical workings of his country estates – which he much preferred to the glamour and glitter of court – earned him the nickname 'Farmer George'.

253 George III – in sharp contrast with previous Hanoverian kings – was a keen reader.

254 His vast library, donated in 1823, formed – along with the Elgin Marbles and Sir Joseph Banks' botanical specimens – a major part of the growing British Museum collection, which opened in 1759.

255 George III never had anything for breakfast except a single cup of tea.

256 One of history's most famous insults was flung at George IV when, in 1813, he attended a 'Dandy Ball' given by Lord Alvanley. George made the mistake of 'cutting' George 'Beau' Brummell, the famously well-dressed society fop. In response to the prince's snub, the unbowed Brummell called loudly: 'Alvanley! Who's your fat friend?'

257 By 1794, George IV's debts had reached an eye-watering £552,000, prompting a general tax on powdered wigs to pay for them.

258 When Sir Frederick Ponsonby proposed to accompany Edward VII wearing a tail-coat, the king replied: 'I thought everyone must know that a short jacket is always worn with a silk hat at a private view in the morning.'

259

Edward VII enjoyed driving cars (an exciting new invention in the Edwardian age) and liked to speed at 60mph – three times the legal limit – on the road from London to Brighton.

260

In 1913, George V and his party set a British record for pheasant slaughter by killing 3,937 birds in a single day's shooting. 'Perhaps we overdid it today,' was the king's thoughtful comment afterwards.

261 One of Edward VIII's few acts as king was to put an end to the tradition – established by Edward VII – that all the clocks at the royal residence of Sandringham should run half an hour fast.

262 Edward VIII was the first monarch to be a qualified pilot.

263 Many of the royal traditions engaged in today are of relatively recent origin. The Trooping of the Colour only began in the reign of Edward VII.

264 The Maundy service at Norwich Cathedral only began with George V.

265 The Official Birthday of the monarch only began with George VI.

266 On being dogged by crowds in London, James I once declared: 'By God's wounds, I will pull down my breeches and they will see my arse!'

267 The stolid Hanoverian George I once remarked 'I hate all Boets and Bainters [poets and painters].'

268 In 1676, Charles II attempted to shut down London's coffee-houses. They were, he said, 'places where the boldest Calumnies and Scandals were raised, and discoursed among a people who know not each other.'

269 Richard I spent just ten months of his ten-year reign in England.

270 'I would sell London if I could find a buyer,' Richard I is supposed to have once remarked.

271 Victoria was not enamoured of the great Liberal Prime Minister W.E. Gladstone: 'He speaks to me as if I was a public meeting,' she sniffed.

272 James I had a fierce hatred of the use of tobacco, declaring it 'a custome lothsome to the eye, hatefull to the Nose, harmefull to the braine, dangerous to the Lungs, and in the blacke stinking fume thereof, neerest resembling the horrible Stigian smoke of the pit that is bottomelesse.'

273 In 1536, Henry VIII ordered that the upper lips of the men of new-conquered Galway were to be clean-shaven.

274 William I attempted to impose a curfew of 8 p.m. on the city of London.

275 In 1404, Henry IV outlawed alchemy – the attempt by early chemists to transform ordinary metals into gold – for fear that it would upset the natural order of things.

276 The law against alchemy wasn't repealed until 1689.

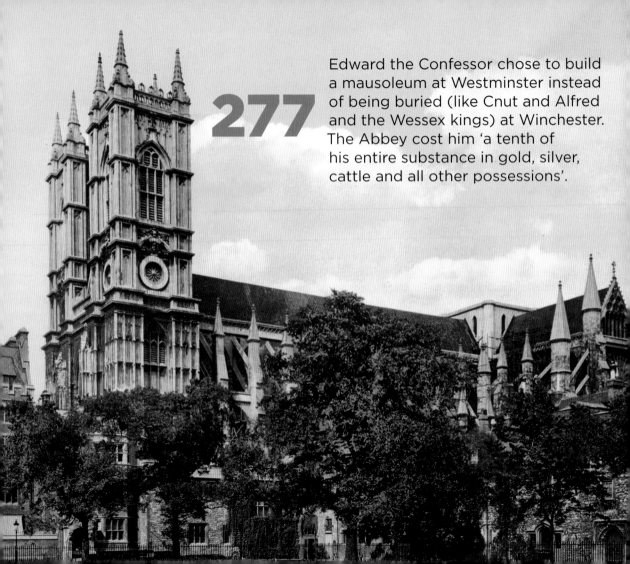

277

Edward the Confessor chose to build a mausoleum at Westminster instead of being buried (like Cnut and Alfred and the Wessex kings) at Winchester. The Abbey cost him 'a tenth of his entire substance in gold, silver, cattle and all other possessions'.

278 It's been suggested that the Abbey was the Confessor's winning move in a game of one-upmanship with his wife Edith, who had rebuilt a nunnery at Wilton.

279 Edward the Confessor – who had spent twenty-five years exiled in France – built Westminster Abbey in the Norman style – just in time for the arrival of the Normans.

280 After all his work on Westminster Abbey, Edward the Confessor was too ill to attend its dedication on 28 December 1065 – despite it being only a few hundred yards from where he lay dying.

281 The first castles in England were built not, as is commonly thought, by William the Conqueror, but by the Normans Richard and Osbert Pentecost. They had been invited over by Edward the Confessor to help him subdue the Welsh.

282 William I did, however, build 500 castles in England during his reign, each a towering symbol of Norman superiority. One of these was the 'White Tower' – now the keep – of the Tower of London.

283 William II built the Great Hall at Westminster, but in the end was underwhelmed by its size. 'It is big enough to be one of my bedchambers,' he muttered grudgingly.

284 Henry III was responsible for massive redevelopments at the Tower of London, creating beautifully decorated lodgings for himself and his queen.

285 Henry III also renovated the Tower's defences.

286 However, Henry III stayed at the Tower just eleven times in his fifty-six-year reign.

287 Edward I spent around £80,000 on his network of castles and other strongholds in North Wales. The mammoth project called for a workforce of some 3,500 men, drawn from all over England.

288

Edward III's £50,000 transformation of Windsor Castle was the most expensive secular construction of the Middle Ages.

CHAPTER
FIVE

Religion, Politics and Money

289 Æthelbert of Kent is remembered as the first English king to convert to Christianity. He did so in around 596.

290 As part of the peace treaty between the Anglo-Saxon king Edmund I and the Viking leader Olaf, Olaf was baptised as Edmund's godson. This was considered perfectly standard practice at the time.

291 Canute the Great was a second-generation Christian.

292 It was actually Christian humility that drove Canute to demonstrate that, for all his courtiers' flattery, he could not turn back the tide – but later chroniclers argued that the stunt in fact proved that Canute was out of his mind.

293 Various saintly accomplishments were attributed to Edward the Confessor, including that when his coffin was opened in 1102 – thirty-seven years after his death – his body was found to be uncorrupted. He was canonised in 1161.

294 The day before William II was killed in a hunting accident in the New Forest, he was visited by a monk from Gloucester. The monk told William of a vision he had seen in which the king attacked Christ and gnawed on his arm – only for Christ to kick him to the ground. William laughed and gave him 100 shillings.

295

A bishop of Rochester calculated that Richard I would have to spend thirty-three years in purgatory as expiation for his sins, and would, as a result, eventually ascend to Heaven in March 1232.

296

In 1318, Edward II was accused of being a changeling imposter by an Exeter tanner named John Powderham. Powderham later testified that he had been persuaded into treason by his pet cat, who was possessed by Satan. He was hanged. So was his cat.

297

In 1419, Joan of Navarre, widow of Henry IV, was put in prison for witchcraft – allowing her stepson Henry V to seize her dowry.

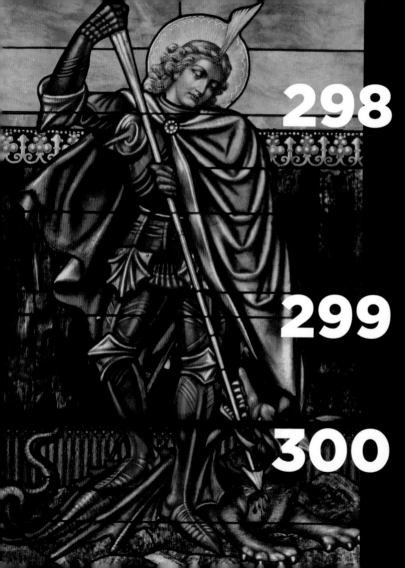

298

Henry VII carried the preserved leg of St George (pictured) through London in a state procession on 22 April 1505. The leg had been given to him by Louis XII of France, and was one of the king's most treasured possessions.

299

Henry VIII was a pious youth. As a teenager he carried around with him a 'bede roll' or prayer guide that included a daily recitation.

300

Anyone who obediently repeated Henry VIII's recitation every day would be granted a total of 52,712 years and 40 days free from purgatory after his death.

301

In 1554, Mary I ordered all bishops to prevent their priests from marrying, and to remove from office those that already were.

302

Mary I's order against priests marrying rather dismayed the Archbishop of York, who wrote asking what he was meant to do with his young wife, whom he had recently married under pressure from Edward VI.

303

Mary earned the nickname 'Bloody Mary' after rebuking a sheriff of Hampshire who cancelled a burning when the intended victim recanted at the stake.

304 Almost 300 Protestant men and women were burned to death during Mary's reign.

305 While under Elizabeth I's reign, more than 200 Catholics were disembowelled or strangled to death.

306 James I believed implicitly in witches and witchcraft. As a young man in Scotland he had, he was sure, encountered a number of witches. In 1597, James I wrote a book on the subject: 'Daemonologie' warned of 'the fearefull aboundinge at this time in this countrie of these detestable slaves of the Devil... witches.'

307 Charles I (pictured) was a firm believer in the power of the monarch's touch to cure the skin disease known as scrofula or 'the king's evil'.

308 The Parliamentarian guards who held Charles after his capture during the Civil Wars nicknamed him 'Stroker'.

309 According to one report, even the king's spittle had once been enough to heal an ailing child.

310 King Charles II was also a prolific 'toucher' for scrofula. He was said to have placed his hands on a total of 92,000 sufferers.

311

So popular was royal 'treatment' for scrofula that, on one occasion, six people hoping to be healed by Charles II ended up being trampled to death in the crowd.

312 The last of the Stuarts, Queen Anne, also did some 'touching'.

313 One of Queen Anne's patients was the infant Samuel Johnson (pictured), who received the royal touch in 1712.

314 William III was less of a devotee. Petitioned by scrofula sufferers, William replied: 'God give you better health and more sense!'

315

English Catholics maintained that the ship that brought George I to England also brought with it a cargo of brown rats. For many years afterwards, Catholics referred to the pestilential animal – which largely supplanted the native black rat – as the 'Hanoverian Rat'.

316

George II had a deeply held belief in vampires, and on more than one occasion rebuked the minister Robert Walpole for speaking lightly of them.

317 George III chastised his son and heir George, Prince of Wales, for slacking in his religious duties and showing insufficient gratitude to 'the Great Creator'.

318 The last words spoken by William IV before his death at Windsor Castle in 1837 are said to have been 'the church, the church…'

319 At 6 a.m. on the morning of 20 June 1837, the Archbishop of Canterbury came in to tell the young Princess Victoria that her uncle William had died, and that she was now Queen. She was still in her dressing-gown.

320 The tradition of the Royal Christmas radio broadcast from Sandringham was instigated in 1932 by George V – and the first message was drafted by Rudyard Kipling.

321 For around two exciting months in 1014, the king of England was a Viking pirate. Sadly, Sweyn Forkbeard died before he could be crowned.

322 Alfred the Great of Wessex (pictured) – not technically a king of England, but certainly an English king – complained that, while his realm was full of excellent, scholarly books, there wasn't anybody left with enough education to read them.

323 The bureaucratic Alfred invented a new kind of lantern that enabled him to work on his papers after nightfall.

324 Æthelred II's bribe to keep out the Vikings, the 'Danegeld', had reached an enormous 48,000lbs of silver by 1012.

325

However, 'in spite of it all, the Danish army went about as it pleased,' the Anglo-Saxon Chronicle reported.

326

Æthelred's nickname, 'the Unready', means that he was without good advisors, or ill-advised.

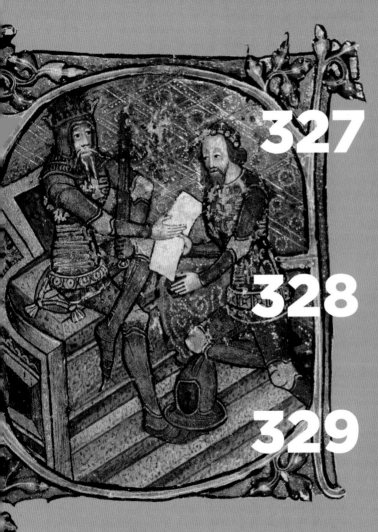

327

Edward III's son Edward of Woodstock – later 'the Black Prince' – was the first man in England to be granted the title 'Duke' (adapted from the French *duc*) when he was made Duke of Cornwall by his father in 1337.

328

Henry V secured a loan of 800 marks from the people of Norfolk by pawning the jewel-studded crown of Richard II, the king usurped by his father Henry IV.

329

Both Henrys had recourse to one of the wealthiest merchants of the age: Richard 'Dick' Whittington made loans totalling £24,000 to Henry IV and £7,500 to Henry V.

330

When Edward de Vere inadvertently broke wind in the presence of Elizabeth I, he was so mortified he left the country for eight years. On his return, Elizabeth's gracious response was: 'My lord, I had forgot the fart.'

331

Charles II chose his wife's Maid of Honour Frances Stuart, Duchess of Richmond, as the model for Britannia on a new coin being struck to mark his naval victories over the Dutch.

332

The Duchess of Richmond remained on British coins for over 300 years, making her final appearance in 2008 on the back of a 50p.

333 George I (pictured) never learned to speak much English and could make no sense of the ranks of the British peerage.

334 However, it was not good practice to point out King George's ignorance: in 1717, the MP William Shippen remarked that George I was 'unacquainted with our language and our constitution'. He was thrown in the Tower for his impertinence.

335 Instead of learning the language himself, George paid for two of his German servants to take English lessons so that they could read the English newspapers for him.

336

As a young monarch, George III (pictured) would have been lost without his mentor the Earl of Bute. In 1759, on entering the Lords, George wrote: 'I am desirous to know whether I am not to put on my hat on taking my seat.'

337

George III also consulted the Earl of Bute regarding the propriety of such highly sensitive issues as 'going to see a production of Henry V' and of giving his wife 'the enamel portrait of himself that she had asked for.'

338

The financial cost of the Napoleonic Wars weighed heavily on the English people. In 1795, in a spirit of sympathy and solidarity, George III and Charlotte ordered that only plain brown bread should be served in the royal household.

339

Charlotte – somewhat optimistically – also sent a recipe for a plain but nourishing potato bread to her son George, the painfully refined Prince of Wales.

340

Diarist George Greville concluded on 18 July 1830: 'Altogether [William IV] seems a kind-hearted, well-meaning, not stupid, burlesque, bustling old fellow, and if he doesn't go mad may make a very decent King.'

341

William IV (pictured) had no desire to be an autocratic monarch. 'I have my view of things,' he said, 'and I tell them to my ministers. If they do not adopt them, I cannot help it. I have done my duty.'

342

In 1865, with Victoria having apparently abandoned her royal duties in order to mourn the loss of Albert, someone affixed to the gates of Buckingham Palace a sign reading: 'These commanding premises to be let or sold, in consequence of the late occupant's declining business.'

343

The names considered as alternatives to Saxe-Coburg-Gotha in 1917 included Brunswick-Luneberg, Guelph, Wettin and D'Este, as well as Plantagenet, York, Lancaster and Fitzroy. The name Saxe-Coburg-Gotha survived in other European monarchies, including the current Belgian Royal Family and the former monarchies of Portugal and Bulgaria.

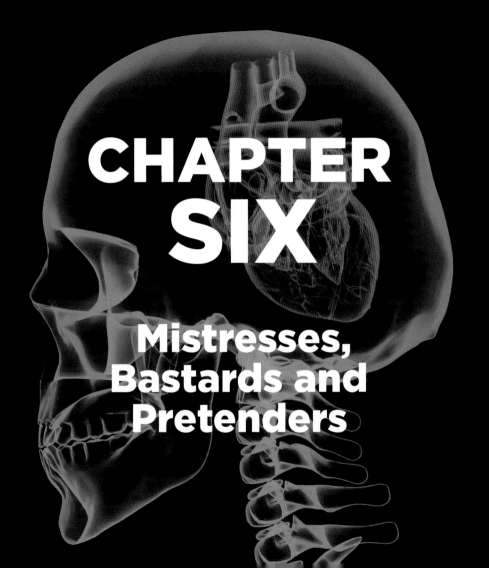

CHAPTER SIX

Mistresses, Bastards and Pretenders

344 Henry II is thought to have had around twelve illegitimate children (to complement the nine legitimate he had with his queen and long-time opponent Eleanor of Aquitaine).

345 Edward III's 'official' mistress, the tiler's daughter Alice Perrers, was accused on the king's death in 1377 of pulling the rings from his fingers before his body was even cold.

346 In February 1669, Catherine of Valois, wife of Henry V, received a visit from Samuel Pepys. It was Pepys' birthday, so to celebrate he gave the queen a kiss on the mouth. At the time he was thirty-six, and the queen was a 268-year-old preserved corpse. 'This was my birth-day, 36 years old [and the day] I did first kiss a Queen,' he cheered in his diary.

347

Edward IV had three mistresses, said by Sir Thomas More to be 'the merriest, the wiliest, and the holiest in the realm'.

348

Richard Plantagenet, the illegitimate son of Richard III, went into hiding following his father's death at the Battle of Bosworth. He worked incognito as a stonemason in a Kent village until his death.

349

Henry VII's reign was plagued by pretenders and imposters. Lambert Simnel, for instance, appeared in 1487 claiming to be the Earl of Warwick, nephew of Edward IV. Henry put him to work turning the spit in the royal kitchens.

350

Henry VIII was more successful at producing children out of wedlock than in it. The king may have sired as many as seven illegitimate children, including five boys.

351 Only one of Henry VIII's illegitimate children was officially acknowledged: Henry Fitzroy ('Fitz' designates illegitimate offspring). He was the son of Elizabeth 'Bessie' Blount.

352 Henry's liaisons with Bessie Blount took place at Jericho House in Essex. Servants there were under orders 'not to hearken or enquire where the king is or goeth' or to discuss 'his late or early going to bed'.

353 Eustace Chapuys, the Imperial Ambassador to England, routinely referred to the infant Elizabeth I as 'the little Bastard'.

354 Charles II used income from the country's new postal services to pay his mistress Barbara De Villiers an annual stipend of £4,700 – a sum that was handed down through the family line until the nineteenth century, when it was commuted for £91,000.

355 It is said that the condom takes its name from a Dr Condom, who invented the prophylactic in an attempt to limit Charles II's output of illegitimate children. George Villiers said of him: 'A king is supposed to be a father to his people, and Charles certainly was father to a good many of them.'

356 Charles acknowledged nine bastard sons (a confusing number of which were called Charles) and five bastard daughters.

357

For ordinary subjects, a king's sexual proclivities were no laughing matter. After the MP Sir John Coventry made a joke in the Commons about the king's fondness for ladies of the stage, he was ambushed on his way home by the king's soldiers, who slit open his nose. This agonising punishment subsequently became known as 'Coventrying'.

358

James Scott, the Duke of Monmouth, was the illegitimate son of Charles II and his mistress Lucy Walter. Talk of a secret marriage and a hidden 'black box' containing the marriage documents led to a rebellion against James II, which was swiftly crushed.

359 Sophia Dorothea, the wife of George I, had an affair with a Swedish aristocrat named Philip von Königsmarck. In her letters to him she assured him that he was a far better lover than George, and said that she wished her husband would be killed in battle.

360 When the affair was discovered, King George I's rival mysteriously vanished – he was probably murdered on the orders of the king's father.

361 Dorothea in turn was banished. George I never spoke of his ex-wife – and the mother of his son and heir George II – again.

362 George I lived with his mistress Engherard Meleusine von der Schulenberg, whom his mother had dubbed 'the Scarecrow'. On the couple's arrival in England, George's new subjects nicknamed her 'the Maypole'.

363 George I was also very close to his half-sister Sophia Charlotte, unkindly nicknamed 'the Elephant'; English scandalmongers went so far as to speculate that he was having an affair with her.

364 The legitimacy of George IV – and, therefore, of all subsequent English monarchs – has been called into question by the persistent rumour that his father, George III, secretly married a Quaker girl called Hannah Lightfoot, the daughter of a Wapping shoemaker, when he was a young man.

365

Caroline of Brunswick (pictured), the estranged wife of Prince Regent George, left England for the continent in August 1814. Feeling unwanted at court, she would remain, she said, simply 'Caroline, a happy, merry soul'.

366

For the next six years, Queen Caroline romped high-spiritedly across Europe while George did his best to pretend that she didn't exist.

367

In 1820 Prince George became King George, and an enquiry was summoned to investigate Queen Caroline's alleged adultery with the Italian Bartolomeo Pergami (pictured opposite). On one occasion the pair evaded curious witnesses by paddling off in a canoe.

368

In the so-called 'Queen's Trial', the British people were staunchly on Caroline's side. Huge numbers of London artisans – bakers, shipwrights, printers, bricklayers – took to the streets to march in support of the queen.

369

Caroline died in 1821. The procession of her body from London to Harwich was attended by huge, ill-tempered crowds. Some resorted to stone-throwing; the troops accompanying the procession responded with gunfire, killing two men.

CHAPTER SEVEN

The King is Dead – Long Live the King!

370 William I, Stephen, Henry I and Henry II were all buried in abbeys they had founded or re-founded.

371 At William's funeral in the monastery of St Stephen, Caen – following his death from an internal rupture – his body burst, emitting a foul stench that sent the mourners running from the building.

372 Henry I famously died from eating 'a surfeit of lampreys' – a kind of slimy, jawless sea-fish – while on a hunting trip.

373 Henry I's body now lies beneath an office block in Reading.

374

Henry's heir, William Adelin, perished aboard the *White Ship*, which sank in the Channel in 1120 with some 300 people aboard.

375

There are two possible reasons why King Stephen, then plain Stephen of Blois, was not also aboard the doomed *White Ship*. One is that he objected to the fact that the crew were all thoroughly drunk (which they certainly were, along with the passengers).

376

Alternatively, King Stephen may have been struck, not by a moment of prudence, but by a severe bout of diarrhoea.

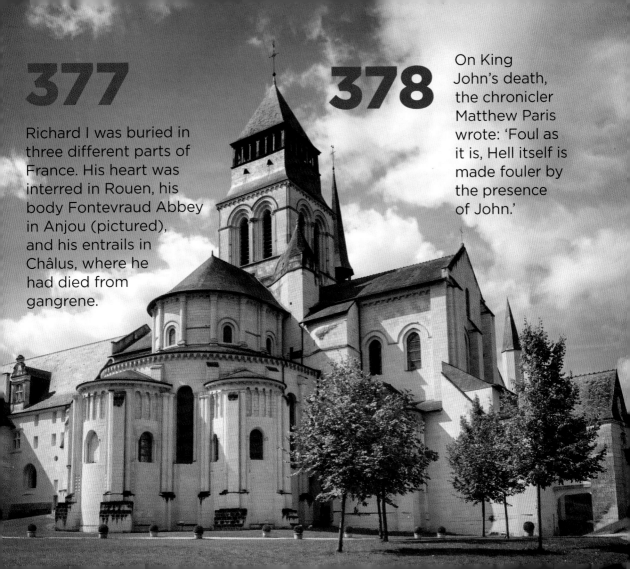

377

Richard I was buried in three different parts of France. His heart was interred in Rouen, his body Fontevraud Abbey in Anjou (pictured), and his entrails in Châlus, where he had died from gangrene.

378

On King John's death, the chronicler Matthew Paris wrote: 'Foul as it is, Hell itself is made fouler by the presence of John.'

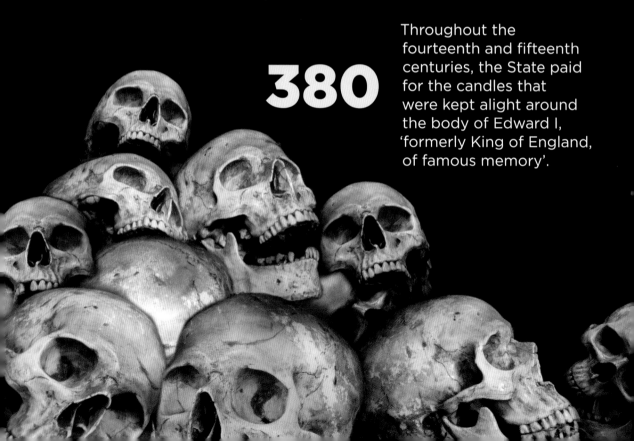

379 On his death-bed, Edward I asked that his body be boiled until the flesh was stripped from his bones, and that his skeleton then be carried at the head of his army until the rebellious Scots were crushed.

380 Throughout the fourteenth and fifteenth centuries, the State paid for the candles that were kept alight around the body of Edward I, 'formerly King of England, of famous memory'.

381 After his lover Piers Gaveston was murdered, Edward II saw to it that he had a decent burial: Gaveston's head was sewn back on, and Edward paid £300 for a gold cloth in which to wrap his body.

382 When Isabella of France, the wife-turned-foe of Edward II, died in 1358, fourteen paupers were paid tuppence a day to pray over her corpse.

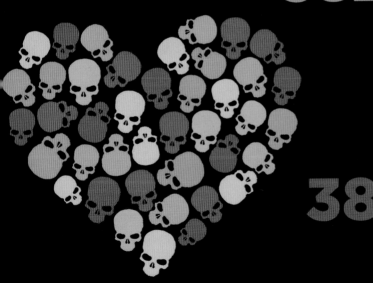

383 In a show of remorse for the spectacular failure of their marriage, Isabella was buried in her wedding gown beside a casket containing the heart of her late husband Edward II.

384 The Black Death arrived in England in 1348, but by then it had already struck a cruel blow against Edward III. Princess Joan, Edward's daughter, had left the country to marry Pedro of Castile just weeks earlier. She succumbed to the terrible pestilence in Bordeaux in August, at the age of just thirteen.

385 According to prophecy, Henry IV was doomed to die 'in Jerusalem'. In fact, he died in the 'Jerusalem Chamber' at Westminster.

386 Henry V died a horrible death from dysentery while on campaign in France.

387 He was not the only one to suffer from this debilitating illness during the Hundred Years' War: English soldiers were known to remove their hose so that they could defecate while on the march.

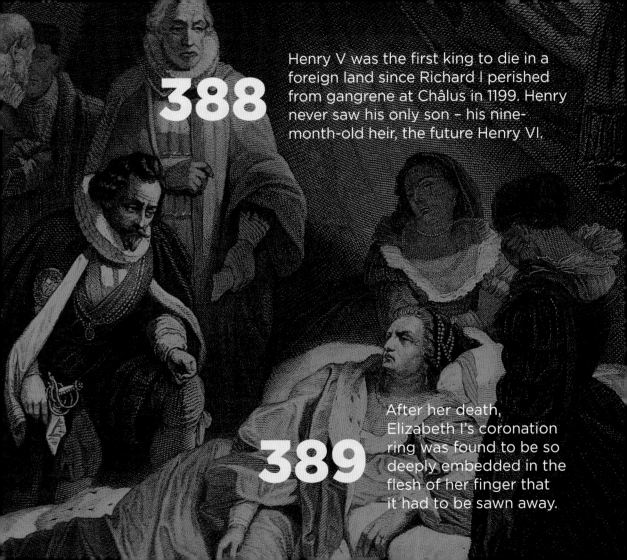

388

Henry V was the first king to die in a foreign land since Richard I perished from gangrene at Châlus in 1199. Henry never saw his only son – his nine-month-old heir, the future Henry VI.

389

After her death, Elizabeth I's coronation ring was found to be so deeply embedded in the flesh of her finger that it had to be sawn away.

390

England's merriest monarch passed away, it is said, with customary good humour. Charles II 'had been, he said, an unconscionable time dying, but he hoped that they would excuse it'.

391

The Protestant William III died in 1702 after falling heavily from his horse. The horse had stumbled over a molehill. Jacobites celebrated by toasting 'the little gentleman in the velvet waistcoat' (i.e the mole).

392 Caroline of Ansbach (pictured), queen of George II, suffered a severe rupture in 1737. The pain was terrible. When a visiting surgeon, bending to tend the queen, inadvertently brushed a lit candle and set his wig on fire, she begged John Rainby, her doctor, to hold her hand so that she could laugh.

393 The dying Caroline told George that he must remarry after her death. The old romantic replied: 'No – I shall have mistresses!'

394 At the funeral of the corpulent George II, the yeomen of the guard carrying the king's coffin were heard to cry out for help, such was the weight of their burden.

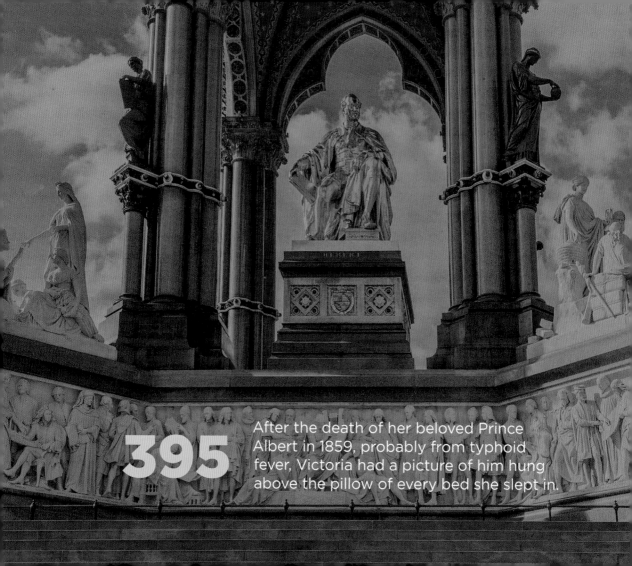

395

After the death of her beloved Prince Albert in 1859, probably from typhoid fever, Victoria had a picture of him hung above the pillow of every bed she slept in.

396

Some famous last words:
Henry II, betrayed by his
sons, said: 'Shame, shame
on a vanquished king!'

397

'An application for some
jelly.' (George III, debilitated
by mental illness.)

398

'Bertie!' (Victoria,
speaking to her son,
the future Edward VII.)

399

'I am very glad.' (Edward VII,
referring not to affairs of state
but to the victory of his horse,
Witch of Air, at Kempton Park.)

400

'God damn you!'
(George V - not,
as is often claimed,
'Bugger Bognor!')

Picture Credits

All images are from the publisher's collection unless otherwise credited.